AMERICAN TRAVELER

NEW ORLEANS

SMITHMARK

This edition first published in 1992 by SMITHMARK
Publishers Inc., 112 Madison Avenue,
New York, New York 10016

ISBN 0-8317-0503-5

Printed and bound in Spain

Writer: Jason Krellenstein
Designer: Ann-Louise Lipman
Design Concept: Lesley Ehlers
Editor: Joan E. Ratajack
Production: Valerie Zars
Photo Researcher: Edward Douglas
Assistant Photo Researcher: Robert V. Hale
Editorial Assistant: Carol Raguso

Title page: New Orleans is the home, heart, and soul of one of America's indigenous art forms, jazz. *Opposite:* Colorful paddle-wheeled riverboats, a New Orleans mainstay since Mark Twain's day, continue to ply the Mississippi, although their preeminence as a source of interstate transportation has considerably diminished. At their peak of use during the mid-nineteenth century, well over a thousand of these slow, serene vessels were operating on the river.

Above: Jeanne d'Arc (left), patron saint of France, was unabashedly appropriated as guardian of the Crescent City by homesick immigrants from France and French Canada. The thriving Port of New Orleans (right), long considered the gateway to the Mississippi, is one of the busiest ports in the continental United States. *Below:* Separated from the Mississippi by enormous glass windows and apparently little else, Riverwalk is an elongated marketplace containing hundreds of shops.

In 1682, an intrepid French Jesuit noble named René Robert Cavelier, Sieur de La Salle, canoed down the Mississippi from the Great Lakes and succeeded in exploring the river's mouth and surrounding delta. He claimed the entire Mississippi Valley for France and graciously named the vast territory *Louisianne* for his patron and financier, Louis XIV, King of France.

After La Salle's death in 1687, Louis sent Pierre Le Moyne, Sieur d'Iberville, up the Mississippi in March 1699. Iberville immediately set to work building a small stockade where he landed near present-day Ocean Springs, Mississippi and dispatched his younger brother, Jean-Baptiste Le Moyne, Sieur de Bienville, to continue exploring the river.

French expansion and colonization all but ground to a halt a mere sixteen years later with the death of Louis XIV in 1715. Because his son, Louis XV, had not reached majority, a council of nobles was appointed to administer the kingdom, with the Duke of Orléans named Regent of France. Orléans's immediate task was to restock the royal coffers, which had been depleted by decades of war and exploration. He recognized immediately that France possessed one as-yet-untapped resource—its vast, wild, southern colony.

The Duke hired a crafty Scottish speculator, ironically named John Law, to promote colonization and encourage investment in the new territory.

Top: Following a humble beginning as a Native American trading post, the Jackson Brewery site, once the source of Jax beer, is now a bustling shopping center. *Right:* Despite the heightened sense of history pervasive throughout New Orleans, lightheartedness and whimsy remain hallmarks of the city's urban landscape.

Law developed a novel idea: He organized a bank to sell shares in the new territory and used the proceeds to replenish the royal treasury. Law was also willing to grant lucrative, long-term trade monopolies to those companies able to glimpse the potential of the marshy, raw colony.

Apparently, however, Law felt little need for candor in his wild descriptions of the territory. He failed to warn prospective settlers of the enormous insect population, of the disproportionate male-to-female ratio, of the voracious alligators, or of the tenacity of the numerous native peoples.

But his venture did have one shining moment. In 1717, the Company of the Indies, formed by Law and led in *Louisianne* by Bienville, chose a site about a hundred miles north of the Gulf along a wide, shallow crescent as a trading post and base from which to organize the colony. Bienville hoped that the bend would provide shelter from powerful, capricious gulf storms. This was probably the site's only advantage; otherwise, it was marshy, insect ridden, and below sea level. Both Law and Bienville had keen senses of protocol; thus, in 1718 they named their settlement New Orleans, simultaneously honoring their patron back in France and the small Loire valley city from which he had come.

New Orleans needed a great deal of work to make it habitable. Labor convicts, imported specifically for the dangerous, dirty

Top to bottom: The Cabildo, a creation of Spanish architect Don Gilberto Guillemard, has served as the seat of the Spanish, French, and American colonial governments, since its completion in 1795. Jackson Square is named for the city's legendary military savior, General Andrew Jackson, who was beloved by the Creole populace. Following his victory over the British in 1815, Jackson humbly received the praise of a grateful citizenry from a window of the Cabildo. *Opposite:* St. Louis Cathedral was originally erected through the generous patronage of Don Almonester y Roxas, a Spanish noble and philanthropist.

The French Market has been the city's traditional center for trade and barter since the late eighteenth century. It is still the site of New Orleans's best bargains in indigenous crafts, domestic and imported produce, and local gossip. *Below:* Colorful boxes of produce from around the world (containing only the occasional tarantula) line the elaborate market. *Opposite:* Garlic and watermelons, a combination unlikely to tempt even the most intrepid epicure, are offered for sale at the French Market. Such a combination is not without logic, however: The city's oppressive humidity and the prolific rumors of vampires can be simultaneously warded off by a single visit to this stall.

work (as opposed to the many other convicts, vagrants, and paupers the Duke of Orléans sent to the colony), were used to drain the swamps, construct levees, and crush and lay oyster shells, all in an effort to stabilize the marshy earth. Bienville had the city laid out in a neat checkerboard pattern and cleared a large parade ground, known as the Place d'Armes, near the river's bank. This part of the city, known as the *Vieux Carré* (Old Quarter), or French Quarter, remains distinctly French in its architecture, street and business names, and local slang and customs.

Some much-needed moral stability was introduced in 1727 with the arrival of a Jesuit missionary, Nicolas de Beaubois, who was accompanied by a band of hardy Ursuline nuns intent upon setting up a school and a hospital. Brought to the territory by Bienville, who was replaced as governor just before the clerics' arrival, Beaubois built a sprawling convent for the industrious sisters on the site of Bienville's former plantation. Graceful and well constructed, the Ursuline Convent miraculously withstood the disastrous fire of 1788 and survives today as the repository for archdiocesan records. The archbishop's chapel, Our Lady of Victory Church, dates from 1845 and stands adjacent to the convent.

In 1762, in a secret treaty after the costly Seven Years' War, Louis XV ceded the distant, still unprofitable *Louisianne* colony to his cousin, Charles III of Spain, as compensation for losses Spain had

Preceding page: Louis Dufilho, believed to be the first licensed pharmacist in America, opened the New Orleans Pharmacy in 1823. *This page, top to bottom:* La Pharmacie Française, now a museum, is complete with an elaborate soda fountain made of brass and Italian marble. The Voodoo Museum is resplendent with occult paraphernalia and objects commemorating Marie Laveau, New Orleans's respected voodoo queen. Much of the French Market was gracefully refurbished in the 1930's under the auspices of the New Deal.

sustained for supporting the defeated France in the war. Charles III didn't send a governor until 1766, when Antonio de Ulloa sailed up the Mississippi with only one ship. The new governor, however, underestimated the resistance of the colonists to Spanish rule. Two years later, the discontented New Orleans citizens, by now a diverse group including Germans, Acadians (or French Canadians), and transplanted continental French, marched through the city by torchlight, calling for Ulloa to flee the city. He apparently took the populace seriously and sneaked out to a Spanish ship that same night. New Orleans is thus distinguished as the first North American city to depose its imported government by insurrection.

The Spaniards were shrewd, experienced, and hardy colonial governors who were not about to be disenfranchised by such a motley crew. King Charles sent one of his finest commanders, General Alejandro O'Reilly, and 2,000 trained Spanish troops to quell the rebellion and reassert Spanish mastery. The ragtag mob wisely chose not to test O'Reilly, and he was easily able to reclaim the territory.

Spanish rule in the ensuing years was practical and benevolent, and the city flourished under the twin influences of French and Spanish culture. The Spaniards were also prolific builders. In 1795, they completed the Cabildo, intended to be the administrative and parliamentary seat of the government, on the Place d'Armes.

Top to bottom: Although proper New Orleanians mourn the passing of absinthe, now illegal in the city because of its renowned ability to dissolve human brain cells, dedicated connoisseurs gather at places such as the Old Absinthe House and continue their diligent search for a substitute. New Orleans's charming street lights recall the civic-minded works of Governor Carondelet, who lit the city with permanent gas lanterns in 1794. Spanish contributions to New Orleans and to its peculiar culture are memorialized in pretty ceramic plaques dotting the buildings of the Vieux Carré.

New Orleans's vivid, exuberant colors pose a stark contrast to the drab landscapes of lesser cities. *Below:* Vieux Carré architecture is distinctly detailed, reflecting the tastes of the individual owners as well as the city's own ineluctable panache.

Of course, the pride of the Vieux Carré dwelling is its garden, redolent with honeysuckle and magnolia. *Below:* The famous Cornstalk Fence is an excellent example of the particular creativity New Orleanians lent to the most pedestrian objects. Strangely, this particular fence was manufactured in Philadelphia. *Opposite:* Delicate, elaborate patterns belie the sturdiness of the wrought iron from which this façade was molded. Balconies such as this are especially favored during the Mardi Gras season; uninhibited revelers have been known to favor passersby with spontaneous, occasionally indiscreet exhibitions.

Gallier Hall, which now houses the mayor's offices, was designed by prolific local architect James Gallier, Sr. Not to be outdone by his accomplished father, James Gallier, Jr. built a splendid mansion, now exactingly restored, on Royal Street. *Below:* Gleaming whitewashed buildings in the Spanish style dot the French Quarter, reminding residents of the industrious but short-lived Spanish stewardship of eighteenth-century *Louisianne*.

Shuttered ground-floor windows and balconies graced with baroque iron fences are characteristic of early Vieux Carré residences. *Below:* Early French colonists shrewdly chose street names calculated to please their noble patrons back home. Royal Street, notable for its genteel antique stores and colorful façades, would certainly have delighted the most discriminating French aristocrat.

Just across the dusty square, the Presbytère was built to house the clergy of the adjacent St. Louis Cathedral. Most impressive, however, is the cathedral itself, which towers over the Place d'Armes. A wealthy Spanish noble, Don Almonester y Roxas, financed the construction of these landmarks. Today, both the Cabildo and the Presbytère, along with three structures from the same era known as the Jackson House, the Creole House, and the Old Arsenal are preserved as part of the Louisiana State Museum.

Political control of *Louisianne* passed back into French hands in 1800 as a result of the Treaty of San Ildefonso, although by then Spanish influence was indelibly stamped upon the city. Apparently adopting the Spanish tradition, the French waited three years before taking possession of the territory. Intermittent war had depleted the French treasury and Napoleon, by then ruler of France, needed a quick infusion of capital to support his army. He sold the enormous *Louisianne* territory to the United States for about four cents an acre. In 1803, less than a month after the French administration returned, New Orleans residents were shocked to see their beloved French tricolor replaced on the Cabildo by the American Stars and Stripes. It was during this period that New Orleans residents popularized the term "Creole" to distinguish citizens of French or Spanish roots from their primitive, northern countrymen.

Top: It is doubtful that the original Folies Bergère in Paris has anything on the New Orleans variety in terms of originality, daring, or unrestrained ribaldry. *Left:* Po'Boys are one of New Orleans's gastronomic traditions: long, drippy, delicious sandwiches probably named for their earliest creators. *Opposite:* Its vaunted southern ambiance notwithstanding, Bourbon Street makes unabashed use of twentieth-century techniques for marketing through neon.

Shuttered ground-floor windows and balconies graced with baroque iron fences are characteristic of early Vieux Carré residences. *Below:* Early French colonists shrewdly chose street names calculated to please their noble patrons back home. Royal Street, notable for its genteel antique stores and colorful façades, would certainly have delighted the most discriminating French aristocrat.

Above: The painstaking detail and unpretensiousness of Royal Street (left) draws fashionable merchants and residents exactly as it did 200 years ago. Gas lanterns (right) are a quaint but efficient light source to augment the dramatic torchlight parades of the carnival season.
Below: Shuttered French windows on a Vieux Carré balcony successfully recall an earlier graceful era.

The New Orleans Wax Museum is a rare peaceful haven in which to contemplate the city's colorful historical tradition and the potent personalities who have shaped it.

Just across the dusty square, the Presbytère was built to house the clergy of the adjacent St. Louis Cathedral. Most impressive, however, is the cathedral itself, which towers over the Place d'Armes. A wealthy Spanish noble, Don Almonester y Roxas, financed the construction of these landmarks. Today, both the Cabildo and the Presbytère, along with three structures from the same era known as the Jackson House, the Creole House, and the Old Arsenal are preserved as part of the Louisiana State Museum.

Political control of *Louisianne* passed back into French hands in 1800 as a result of the Treaty of San Ildefonso, although by then Spanish influence was indelibly stamped upon the city. Apparently adopting the Spanish tradition, the French waited three years before taking possession of the territory. Intermittent war had depleted the French treasury and Napoleon, by then ruler of France, needed a quick infusion of capital to support his army. He sold the enormous *Louisianne* territory to the United States for about four cents an acre. In 1803, less than a month after the French administration returned, New Orleans residents were shocked to see their beloved French tricolor replaced on the Cabildo by the American Stars and Stripes. It was during this period that New Orleans residents popularized the term "Creole" to distinguish citizens of French or Spanish roots from their primitive, northern countrymen.

Top: It is doubtful that the original Folies Bergère in Paris has anything on the New Orleans variety in terms of originality, daring, or unrestrained ribaldry. *Left:* Po'Boys are one of New Orleans's gastronomic traditions: long, drippy, delicious sandwiches probably named for their earliest creators. *Opposite:* Its vaunted southern ambiance notwithstanding, Bourbon Street makes unabashed use of twentieth-century techniques for marketing through neon.

Napoleon House was intended as a sanctuary for the deposed emperor following his rescue from St. Helena by loyal New Orleans patriots; unfortunately, Napoleon died before the wild plan could be effected. *Below, left:* The Absinthe House is mute testimony to the days when wormwood was the intoxicant of choice in the Vieux Carré. *Right:* The Court of the Two Sisters offers a romantic dining experience in its secluded, peaceful garden, considered one of the Vieux Carré's finest. *Opposite:* Bourbon Street is actually named for the powerful French dynasty, and not for the powerful American corn liquor so often in evidence in the French Quarter.

Preceding page:: The Chosen Few Marching Band, and countless others like it, faithfully maintain the New Orleans tradition of live, innovative, and passionate street music. *This page, right:* Mardi Gras is particularly beloved by the local citizenry because it permits—even compels—unself-conscious participation. *Below:* Street theater is a popular and inexpensive New Orleans mainstay that recalls the city's early continental roots.

There is no honor greater than a New Orleans jazz funeral. The eulogy at this unique ceremony is delivered in music, arguably the city's truest, most indigenous language. *Below:* The city's unparalled musical heritage is built and sustained through the generations with pride. *Opposite:* Marie Laveau, the city's voodoo queen, is credited with two tombs in St. Louis Cemetery No. 1. Popular rumor has it that she likes them both.

New Orleans's remarkable sense of history is not confined to the previous century: A skyscraper provides a modern backdrop for the city's monument to veterans of the Vietnam War. *Below:* A whimsical metal sculpture brightens what might have been a grim urban plaza. This one is an interpretation of a local "krewe," or Mardi Gras parade club.

the city's second greatest religious tradition. The museum's gift shop is one of the few place that sells *gris-gris,* or charms, which can be imbued with various powers according to the purchaser's needs or tastes.

For all its daily excitement, however, New Orleans most of the time is but a pale imitation of New Orleans during the sustained madness of the Mardi Gras season. Although based on the *Carnivale* introduced by the colonial French, Mardi Gras was actually rejuvenated by the Americans after the Spaniards had banned masked affairs as a security precaution. The first modern Mardi Gras began as a spontaneous march through the Vieux Carré by a group of New Year's Eve merrymakers in 1830. Enjoying themselves immensely, these pioneers vowed to make the parade an annual affair.

Eventually, the group decided their parade should be held just prior to the Lenten season; they named their band the Mysticke Krewe of Comus, after Ben Jonson's God of Good Cheer. The parades evolved into a series of elaborate, torchlit affairs beginning in late January and culminating sharply at midnight on Fat Tuesday, the day before forty days of fasting begin on Ash Wednesday. At that time, New Orleans police officers on horseback link their batons and ride through the streets, sweeping them clean and leaving a very eerie echo over the empty French quarter.

Top: The New Orleans Museum of Art has one of the finest collections of Impressionist and Modern works in the entire South. Edouard Degas, whose brothers lived and worked in the Cotton Exchange, professed a great love for the city's relaxed lifestyle and has been rewarded with an entire gallery devoted to his works. *Right:* The Audubon Zoo, located in lush Audubon Park, is a popular favorite with both New Orleans's society and college students. On any given day, crowds of students may be seen at the comprehensive primate section, gibbering at the puzzled animals.

The Mardi Gras Fountain, near gigantic Lake Pontchartrain, is illuminated with traditional Mardi Gras purple, green, and gold lights, appearing to the uninitiated as a fountain of delightfully colored, possibly magical, elixirs.

The Lake Pontchartrain Causeway, here stretching seemingly into infinity, is, at 24 miles long, the world's largest bridge. The causeway spans the shallow lake, connecting Orleans and Jefferson parishes.

Above: Hauntingly beautiful, Metairie Cemetery (left), was at one time a popular racetrack. Among a great many other famous residents, Jessie Arlington, one of the city's most famous madams, rests in Metairie Cemetery. Her tomb (right) is thought to depict the fateful night that she was turned away from her father's home, after which she was forced to go into business for herself. *Below:* These unusual individual crypts were popularized in Louisiana as an antidote to the persistent flooding and soil erosion so damaging to low-lying cemeteries. *Opposite:* Although respect for history and myth is characteristic of much of the city, New Orleanians have never been especially choosy about precisely whose history they make use of. Metairie Cemetery here borrows from the Arthurian legends of old England.

Tulane's president traditionally lives at One Audubon Place, an airy, columned mansion on a private street unchallenged as New Orleans's finest and most exclusive. Directly across from the university is Audubon Park, site of New Orleans's delightful Zoological Garden. The park is a lush expanse of beautiful trees, ponds, and grassy fields abutting the levee protecting the Garden District from the Mississippi.

Little known to outsiders, the Lakeside district, named for enormous Lake Pontchartrain, harbors the city's largest park, aptly named City Park, as well as other treasures. The park was at one time the sight of regular duels between passionate Creole gentlemen, and the impressive oak trees guarding the entrance to New Orleans Museum of Art are known as the Dueling Oaks. On nearby Lakeshore Drive, the Mardi Gras fountain sprays water colored in the unlikely combination of purple, gold, and green, the Mardi Gras colors.

No account of New Orleans could pretend completeness without a discussion of the cuisine. The development of New Orleans cooking closely tracks the gradual blending of cultures that shapes the city. Cornmeal bread, a native legacy, and local fish and crustaceans were staples of early settler diets. To the relatively sophisticated palates of French and Spanish colonists, the Acadians introduced fiery spices.

Top to bottom: In response to the discreet, cloistered homes of the French Quarter, Garden District settlers built imposing, classical mansions on trim, wide grounds. The whimsical influences of continental New Orleans are not lost on impressive uptown homes: Here, an imposing classical mansion is softened by a coat of pink paint. Uptown residents were generally unimpressed with the tiny plots upon which the opulent Vieux Carré homes were built. Consequently, many of the finest Garden District houses were erected on large, open spaces easily visible to passersby. *Opposite:* Although the Greek influence is readily perceptible in the Garden District, each home is unique.

Enormous trees of indeterminate age festooned with exotic looking Spanish moss complement this rather rambling uptown house. *Below:* Even the smaller New Orleans homes radiate their owner's pride as well as the pervasive Grecian influence.

The Fenner House, on First Street, was occupied for a time by a Union general during the Civil War. Ironically, Jefferson Davis used this house frequently in his idle years following the war and died there during a visit to the city in 1889. *Below:* Christ Church Cathedral is one of the oldest Protestant houses of worship in this traditionally Catholic city. This very gothic, imposing structure was completed in the 1880's.

JEFFERSON DAVIS
BORN AT FAIRVIEW, KY. JUNE 3, 1808.
U. S. ARMY   1828 — 1835
SERVED IN BLACK HAWK WAR
                                    1845 — 1846
CONGRESSMAN U. S.
COLONEL MISSISSIPPI VOLUNTEERS IN WAR WITH MEXICO
RENDERED GALLANT SERVICE IN TAKING MONTEREY
AND BUENA VISTA WHERE HE WAS SEVERELY WOUNDED.
                                    1847 — 1851
SENATOR U. S.   1853 — 1857
SECRETARY OF WAR U. S.   1857 — 1861
SENATOR U. S.   1861 — 1865
PRESIDENT C. S. A.   1865 — 1867
PRISONER FORTRESS MONROE
ERECTED BY LADIES CONFEDERATE MEMORIAL ASSOCIATION
MAY 17, 1930.

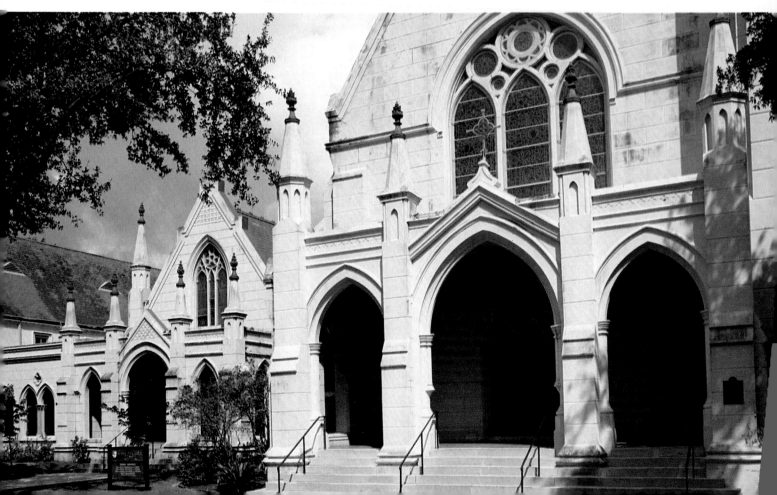

The resulting cuisine emphasizes local delicacies. Crayfish, called crawfish within Louisiana, are tiny, mud-crawling shellfish akin to the lobster. Crawfish boils are always messy, delicious, and unrestrained fun; neophytes attempting to find the edible part of the little creatures are urged to "suck the head and squeeze the tip." Oysters are a popular bar snack. Gumbo, a thick, unlikely mixture of shellfish, sausage, rice, tomatoes, and okra in a chicken stock, should never taste the same in two restaurants. Of course, casual meals are always washed down with Dixie Beer, New Orleans's own beer made from Mississippi River water.

What then is the true sum of this eclectic metropolis? It is a city of grace, of proud tradition, of unrestrained ribaldry, of startling beauty. Alone of American cities, New Orleans has suceeded in maintaining a palpable European charm; no other city so reverently celebrates its diverse history. If the Mississippi River is the lifeblood of the South, New Orleans is surely its steamy, chaotic, joyous heart.

Top: The essence of New Orleans is the Mardi Gras parade. Two-dimensional representations or written descriptions cannot begin to capture the scope, pageantry, or excitement generated by the lumbering, confectionary floats. *Left:* The colors, sounds, and emotion of the parades are refreshingly immune to the teeming influences of commercialism. In fact, even lifelong residents are hard pressed to explain the allure of the worthless but nevertheless prized trinkets tossed to the expectant crowds by gaudy revelers aboard their cartoonish floats. *Opposite:* Mardi Gras parades are organized by krewes. Far more highly prized than even the slippery, elusive aluminum doubloons tossed off the floats are invitations to the elegant balls given by the respective krewes during Lent. Eschewing the theme of atonement common to Lenten rituals, Mardi Gras balls are indulgent, glittering evocations of New Orleans's golden era.

This page: Of course, uninhibited self-expression is not only appreciated but required during the heady days of carnival. And even the most ordinary New Orleanian is given to fanciful costumes and elaborate headgear. Residents engage in subtle but keen competition to present the most fantastic, the most obscure, and the most whimsical costumes possible. In fact, while these gentlemen appear to be having a tremendous amount of fun, they are actually fully engaged in trying to discern the meanings of their elaborate costumes. *Opposite:* This seemingly intrusive feathered behemoth is actually a respected, even celebrated, member of his krewe.

Index of Photography

All photographs courtesy of The Image Bank, except where indicated *.

Page Number	Photographer	Page Number	Photographer
Title Page	Eddie Hironaka	30 Bottom	Lou Jones
3	Janeart Ltd.	31	Philip Gould*
4 Top Left	Luis Castañeda	32-33	Paul Nehrenz
4 Top Right	Paul Nehrenz	34 (2)	Paul Nehrenz
4 Bottom	Ronald R. Johnson/Stockphotos, Inc.*	35	Mark E. Gibson*
5 Top	Andy Caulfield	36 (3)	Luis Castañeda
5 Bottom	Guido Alberto Rossi	37 Top	Luis Castañeda
6 Top & Center	Luis Castañeda	37 Bottom	Joe Azzara
6 Bottom	Sean Smith/Stockphotos, Inc.*	38	Luis Castañeda
7	Andy Caulfield	39	Al Satterwhite
8 (2)	Luis Castañeda	40 Top	Luis Castañeda
9	Luis Castañeda	40 Bottom	Andy Caulfield
10	Alfredo Tessi	41 Top	Audrey Gibson*
11 Top	Louis H. Jawitz	41 Bottom	Janeart Ltd.
11 Center	Luis Castañeda	42 Top	Alfredo Tessi
11 Bottom	Janeart Ltd.	42 Bottom	Marie Celino*
12 Top	Robert Holmes*	43 (2)	Janeart Ltd.
12 Center	Eddie Hironaka	44	Luis Castañeda
12 Bottom	Ross M. Horowitz/Stockphotos, Inc.*	45	Guido Alberto Rossi
13 Top	Luis Castañeda	46 Top (2)	Marie Celino*
13 Bottom	Harald Sund	46 Bottom	Audrey Gibson*
14 Top	Janeart Ltd.	47	Marie Celino*
14 Bottom	Luis Castañeda	48-49	Murray Alcosser
15	Nick Nicholson	50 (3)	Murray Alcosser
16 (2)	Luis Castañeda	51	Murray Alcosser
17 Top	Jake Rajs	52	Philip Gould*
17 Bottom	Luis Castañeda	53	Ronald R. Johnson/ Stockphotos, Inc.*
18 Top Left	Luis Castañeda	54	Mark E. Gibson*
18 Top Right & Bottom	Audrey Gibson*	55	Luis Castañeda
19	Louis H. Jawitz	56 Top	Robert Holmes*
20 (2)	Joe McNally	56 Center	Mark E. Gibson*
21	Joe McNally	56 Bottom	Don Klumpp
22 Top	Philip Gould*	57	Ronald R. Johnson/ Stockphotos, Inc.*
22 Bottom (2)	Ronald R. Johnson/ Stockphotos, Inc.*	58 Top	Philip Gould*
23	Andy Caulfield	58 Bottom	Mark E. Gibson*
24-25	Joe McNally	59 (2)	Luis Castañeda
26 Top	Eddie Hironaka	60 Top	Luis Castañeda
26 Center	Andy Caulfield	60 Bottom	Andrea Pistolesi
26 Bottom	Peter Beney	61	Luis Castañeda
27	Jake Rajs	62 Top Left	Marie Celino*
28	Philip Gould*	62 Top Center & Bottom	Luis Castañeda
29 Top	Philip Gould*		
29 Bottom	Joe McNally	62 Top Right	Janeart Ltd.
30 Top	Marie Celino*	63	Luis Castañeda